Stoicism for the Modern Teen

Rajat Akre

ISBN: 978-93-343-8386-7

DEDICATION

For you, my newborn child, may you grow with courage, wisdom, justice, and self-control.
May these pages guide you through every storm and celebration alike, lighting the path to who you choose to become.

And to every teen reading this: the world awaits your strength and compassion.

May these lessons help you stand steady, speak kindly, and act with purpose—today, tomorrow, and always.

CONTENTS

ACKNOWLEDGMENTS

This book would not exist without the wisdom, encouragement, and collaboration of many extraordinary people:

To my parents, whose steady love and belief in possibility shaped every page of my life and work—thank you for teaching me that character is built one choice at a time.

To the teachers, mentors, and coaches who guided curious minds with patience, challenged assumptions with kindness, and modeled the virtues this book explores—your example lights the way for young seekers.

To the teenagers who shared their stories, struggles, and triumphs—your honesty inspired these lessons, and your courage reminds me daily why this work matters.

To my editors and design team, whose care for clarity and beauty translated these ideas into a journey both accessible and uplifting—your craftsmanship made these principles shine.

To friends and colleagues who debated concepts late into the night and offered invaluable feedback—your insights strengthened every chapter.

To my child, just arriving in this world—may these pages be a companion on your journey, and may you grow into the fullest expression of your potential.

And finally, to the ancient Stoics—Epictetus, Seneca, Marcus Aurelius—and all who have carried their message forward: thank you for showing us how to stand firm amid life's storms and turn every obstacle into an opportunity for growth.

Chapter 1: Who Am I? The Quest for Identity

"You have power over your mind - not outside events. Realize this, and you will find strength." - Marcus Aurelius

---

The Mirror Question

Maya scrolls through a mosaic of perfection—glowing selfies, vacation sunsets, GPA flexes. Her own profile looks bright and fearless, the result of many retakes and edits. When she lowers the phone, the mirror returns a different picture: tired eyes, a tense jaw, a mind buzzing with comparisons.

The gap between screen and glass poses a stubborn question: Who am I, really? She feels suspended between what people see and what she feels, between who she was and who she hopes to be. The tension lingers like a low hum under everything else she does.

A question this large needs steadier ground than likes and labels—ground the Stoics spent centuries mapping.

Concept: Logos (Reasoned Order)

Definition: The Stoics believed the world runs on reason and that each person holds a spark of it; identity grows by living in line with that reason.

Teen Example: Instead of asking "Do they like me?" ask "Am I acting like the person I respect?"

Ancient Wisdom, Modern Noise

Long before social feeds, reputations were public currency. Emperors kept journals to steady their minds. Teachers like Epictetus drew a line through life: what's up to us and what isn't. Maya's world feels new, but her struggle is old.

She thinks of metrics—follows, test scores, dress codes of friendship. If those define her, she's riding a shifting tide. If identity rests on choices and values, she holds the wheel. She breathes in and lists what she can steer today: how she speaks to her brother, how she studies tonight, what she posts—or doesn't.

When control is clarified, self-respect becomes possible regardless of the crowd.

Concept: Dichotomy of Control

Definition: Build identity on what you can govern—thoughts, values, choices—not on what you can't—opinions, trends, outcomes.

Teen Example: You can't force comments to be kind; you can choose to post with honesty and log off on time.

The Performance Trap

Marcus, a senior at Maya's school, lives inside a role: star quarterback. Photos, trophies, headlines—his name seems fused to a jersey. Then a knee injury ends his season. Without the role, silence rushes in.

At first he feels hollow. Slowly, another idea arrives: the role can change; the person practicing courage doesn't have to. He visits practice to support teammates. He studies plays, helps a sophomore with footwork, shows up to rehab on rough days. He begins to sense a self that outlasts the scoreboard.

Roles are stages; character is the actor who can walk from one stage to the next.

Concept: Roles vs. Nature

Definition: We play many roles, but our core is a moral agent capable of wisdom, justice, courage, and self-control.

Teen Example: "I'm more than my subject rank or my starter spot; I'm the kind of person who shows up with effort and respect."

Becoming, Not Arriving

Sarah's home splits into two apartments. Labels form quickly: "child of divorce," "the quiet one." She almost accepts them as permanent until a counselor asks, "What kind of person will you practice being this month?" Sarah picks three words: kind, reliable, brave. She acts them out in small ways—helping her younger brother with homework, texting a friend first, asking a teacher for help.

Days accumulate. The situation still hurts, but her choices stitch a sturdier story. She realizes identity isn't a title; it's a trail of actions repeated on purpose.

The person we become is built one choice at a time—especially on hard days.

Concept: Virtue as Skill

Definition: Virtues are trainable habits—like muscles—that grow through repeated use.

Teen Example: Courage gets stronger every time you speak the truth kindly when it would be easier to stay quiet.

Core Principles for Building Resilience and Character

At the heart of Stoic practice are four foundational principles that guide teens in developing inner strength and wise living.

Dichotomy of Control

This principle teaches that some things are within our control—like our thoughts, values, choices, and effort—while many others, such as others' opinions, the past, algorithms, and outcomes, are not. Learning to distinguish clearly between what we can govern and what we cannot helps conserve energy and focus. A simple, effective exercise is to visualize this as three concentric circles representing control, influence, and no control. Direct your attention first to the center circle—your direct control—and let go of unnecessary worry about the outer rings.

Discipline of Assent

Not every thought deserves your agreement or emotional energy. Many mental impressions are fleeting or distorted. This principle encourages a mindful pause before accepting thoughts as true. For example, if a harsh thought arises—"I'm not enough"—ask yourself: Is there evidence to support this? Is it helpful? Is it within my power to change? If the answer to any is no, consciously reframe the thought with kinder, more balanced perspectives.

The Four Cardinal Virtues

Stoicism centers on cultivating four key virtues that nurture moral character:

Wisdom: Practicing sound judgment

Justice: Treating others fairly and with respect

Courage: Doing what is right even in the face of fear

Temperance: Exercising self-control and moderation

To integrate these virtues into daily life, choose one virtue to focus on each week and identify a specific, manageable action that reflects it. Small, consistent practice builds lasting character.

Inner Citadel

This principle envisions the mind as a fortress—a resilient inner sanctuary fortified through reflection and routine. Daily practices such as setting a purposeful intention each morning and reviewing your actions kindly each evening help protect this mental stronghold. Treat these moments of self-reflection like training sessions—regular, purposeful, and essential to your daily growth.

Practical Exercises (with why it helps)

Morning Identity Check — Ask, "What kind of person will I practice being today?" Choose one behavior to match. Why it helps: A clear aim shapes choices before pressure arrives.

Three Circles Map — List items in control, influence, and no-control rings. Why it helps: Cuts wasted effort and reduces anxiety.

Role Reflection — Write your current roles and one virtue to bring to each this week. Why it helps: Prevents over-identifying with a single role.

Character Journal — Note one moment of alignment and one of misalignment daily. Why it helps: Turns days into data for growth.

Obstacle Reframe — When a setback hits, ask, "What quality is this training?" Why it helps: Converts pain into purposeful practice.

Reflection Questions

- Which labels do you use for yourself that someone else could take away—and which virtues no one can remove?
- When was the last time you reacted for approval rather than from values? How would you replay it differently?
- Which virtue would change your week the most? What's one action to practice it today?

- In your three circles, what will you stop feeding attention to this month?
- What would your closest friend say your consistent actions reveal about who you are becoming?

"Identity isn't something found online—it's something forged by choices aligned with values, repeated until they feel like you."

Chapter 2: The Power of Your Mind

"You have power over your mind - not outside events. Realize this, and you will find strength." - Marcus Aurelius

"It's not what happens to you, but how you react to it that matters."
- Epictetus

The Cafeteria Replay

Alex sits at the edge of the lunch crowd, fork idle, thoughts racing back to the morning's chemistry exam. The questions had looked familiar in the notebook and strange on the page. Study hours didn't translate when the clock started. Now, three hours later, the mind still replays missed steps and blank spaces.

The body joins in: tight shoulders, a knotted stomach, shallow breaths. Each thought adds another layer—If I failed, I'll wreck my GPA. If my GPA slips, college is over. If college is over, my future is gone. A single test grows into a catastrophe.

Across the room, Jordan unpacks the same exam with less panic. It was hard. Some guesses. No drama. Jordan decides to ask Ms. Rodriguez for help and plans a new study block.

Two students faced the same event, but their inner stories led to two very different afternoons.

Impressions vs. Judgments

Definition: Events give us impressions (raw facts); our judgments about those impressions create most of our feelings and actions.

Teen Example: "I missed questions on a test" is an impression; "I'm a failure and my future is ruined" is a judgment.

The First Pause

On the walk to class, Alex notices how thoughts leap ahead faster than footsteps. A small decision appears: keep replaying, or test the story. Alex breathes in for four counts, out for six, and names the facts: There was a test. I struggled on several questions. I studied. I felt nervous. Naming facts slows the spiral.

A new question follows: What is in my hands right now? Alex can review mistakes after school, ask Ms. Rodriguez for feedback, and plan two short practice sessions before the quiz on Friday. The grade hasn't arrived, but the plan has.

The pause doesn't erase worry, but it opens a door from panic to action.

Discipline of Assent

Definition: Before agreeing with a thought, examine it—accept the useful, reject the distorted, and choose a wiser response.

Teen Example: When the mind says "Everyone finished easily," ask: Do I know that? Even if some did, what can I do next?

Brains Under Construction

That afternoon, Emma walks into a packed club meeting and feels heat rise to her face. Old thoughts appear: They're staring. I don't belong. She remembers her practice—notice, name, and nudge. Notice the fear. Name the thought. Nudge the story toward truth: People are busy with their own conversations. Nervous is normal. She stays, speaks once, and the fear shrinks.

Attention, practiced daily, becomes a quiet strength—like training a muscle that keeps you steady when moments wobble.

Inner Citadel

Definition: A trained mind becomes a safe center that pressure can't easily shake.
Teen Example: Presentations still bring nerves, but with practiced breathing and a simple plan, you deliver anyway.

Core Principles

These foundational principles serve as a compass for guiding teens toward resilience, clarity, and virtue in everyday life.

Dichotomy of Control

Recognizing what is within your control—and what is not—is key to staying balanced. Your thoughts, choices, and effort are wholly yours to govern, while others' opinions, the weather, or exam curves fall outside your command. A practical way to embody this is by drawing three concentric circles symbolizing: things you control, things you can influence, and things beyond your reach. Direct your energy starting from the center—your own control—and gently release concern for what lies beyond.

Discipline of Assent

Not every mental impression deserves your unquestioning belief. Before accepting a thought, especially stressful or negative ones, pause and reflect.

- Use the acronym STOP:
- Stop what you're doing
- Take a breath for calm
- Observe the thought impartially
- Proceed on purpose with a balanced response

This practice trains your mind to replace distorted or unhelpful thoughts with clearer, more constructive ones.

Four Cardinal Virtues

Stoicism highlights four core virtues that shape strong character and sound decision-making:

Wisdom: Making thoughtful and informed choices
Justice: Acting with fairness and respect toward others
Courage: Doing the right thing, even when scared
Temperance: Exercising self-control and moderation

Focus on one virtue each week. Set a simple, daily action aligned with that virtue to bring it alive in your life.

Inner Citadel

Imagine your mind as a fortress—protected by daily habits of reflection and intention. Building this inner citadel means taking just a few minutes each morning to set your aim and a few more each evening to review your day. Over a week, this consistent practice "bricks" a resilient mental core that steadies you through life's challenges.

Practical Exercises (with why it helps)

Five-Count Breathing — Inhale 4, exhale 6 for two minutes. Why it helps: Calms the nervous system so the thinking brain can re-engage.

Thought Record — Write the situation, automatic thought, evidence for/against, balanced replacement. Why it helps: Turns vague fear into testable ideas.

Perspective Timer — Set three random alarms; each time ask, "Helpful? In my control?" Why it helps: Builds micro-habits of attention during real life.

Test Debrief Template — After any assessment: three things I understood, two gaps, one next action. Why it helps: Converts outcomes into a plan.

Emotional Weather Report — "Anger is present" instead of "I am angry." Why it helps: Creates space between you and the feeling so you can choose a response.

Reflection Questions

- What was your last strong impression? Which judgments did you add, and how did they change your mood?
- Which thinking trap snags you most: all-or-nothing, catastrophizing, mind reading, fortune telling, personalization?
- Where could a 2-minute pause improve your day—before texting back, opening results, or stepping on stage?
- Which virtue, if practiced this week, would change your choices the most—and what single action will you take?
- What one part of your digital routine will you adjust to protect your attention?

"You can't command every event, but you can train the story you tell about it—and that story shapes what you do next."

CHAPTER 3: WHAT YOU CAN AND CANNOT CONTROL

"Some things are in our control and others not. Things in our control are opinion, pursuit, desire, aversion, and, in a word, whatever are our own actions. Things not in our control are body, property, reputation, command, and, in one word, whatever are not our own actions." - Epictetus

"To make the best of what is in our power, and take the rest as it occurs." -Epictetus

---

The Eye of the Hurricane

Zoe sits cross-legged on the floor, back against the bed, phone buzzing on the carpet. The party videos loop in her mind: Rachel laughing with Brittany, the clink of soda cans, a sparkler in slow motion. The sting is sharp and personal. Thoughts stack fast and absolute—Everyone is talking. I have no real friends. This year is ruined.

Her chest tightens. A dozen responses crowd the doorway: a furious text, a vague story meant to bite, a plan to disappear at school. She opens Messages, then closes it. In the quiet between pings, a small, stubborn question appears: What part of this can I actually steer?

When the storm feels total, the first lifeline is a boundary line.

The Great Division

Definition: Peace begins when we divide life into what is ours to govern (thoughts, choices, actions) and what is not (other people, outcomes, past).

Teen Example: You can't control who invites you; you can control how you respond and whom you invest in next.

Mapping the Circles

Zoe opens her notebook and draws three rings. In the center she writes: words I choose, people I check on, how I carry myself tomorrow. In the middle: my part in friendships, how I clear rumors, where I spend time. In the outer ring: Rachel's decisions, Brittany's posts, everyone's opinions.

The picture is simple and steadying. Rage loosens a notch. She drafts a calm message to Rachel: "Saw the stories. I felt left out. Can we talk tomorrow?" She deletes a snarky caption she almost posted and sets her phone to Do Not Disturb.

Clarity doesn't erase hurt, but it turns hurt into a plan that fits inside your hands.

Sphere of Control

Definition: Focus energy on the inner circle (complete control), apply effort in the middle (influence), and accept the outer (no control).

Teen Example: You can't control comments on a post, but you can control your screen time and whether you reply with grace or not at all.

School Halls and Real Tests

The next morning, lockers slam and chatter spills down the hall. Zoe's stomach flutters, but she rehearsed her line: Speak from values, not from heat. When she and Rachel finally meet by the water fountain, words don't feel easy, but they arrive: "I was hurt. I want to understand." Rachel stumbles through an apology mixed with confusion. Brittany's rumor started the drift; the party invite got messy.

The conversation doesn't solve everything. It does something better—it shows Zoe she can be the kind of friend she respects, even when the scene is awkward. At lunch, she chooses a table where she feels seen. The circles map sits in her pocket, inked and warm.

Results may vary; character can be consistent.

Right Action over Outcome

Definition: Doing the next wise thing matters more than controlling what happens after.

Teen Example: You can't force a perfect talk, but you can choose honesty and calm, and that choice is success on your side of the line.

Wider Than One Moment

Elsewhere, Marcus refreshes a college portal that hasn't posted decisions yet, and Sarah studies for a test she can't predict. Each faces the same fork: spend energy on the unknown, or invest it in what they can do now. Marcus drafts a better essay paragraph; Sarah practices two problem types she always mix up. They feel the same nerves, and they keep moving anyway.

Zoe walks home under a fading sky, feeling both tender and strong. She can't edit last night. She can choose tonight's call, tomorrow's habits, the tone of her voice when she's tired. The storm hasn't vanished. She's learning to stand in the calm center.

Mastery of the small, controllable things often changes the big picture more than chasing the big picture directly.

The Paradox of Letting Go

Definition: Releasing control of outcomes frees energy for effort, which often improves outcomes.

Teen Example: Stop trying to engineer who likes you; pour into being kind, reliable, and real—people notice.

Practical Exercises

The Three Circles Sketch — Draw inner/influence/outer for any stressor. Why it helps: Turns overwhelm into a plan with clear lanes for action.

Serenity Pause — Breathe in 4, out 6; name one controllable next step. Why it helps: Calms physiology so judgment can lead.

My-Part Checklist — For tough tasks, list "effort, attitude, honesty, follow-through" and tick them off. Why it helps: Reframes success around controllables.

Response Template — "I can't control X. I can control Y. So my action is Z." Why it helps: Converts rumination into behavior.

Energy Audit — For one week, log 3 daily worries and label them inner/middle/outer. Why it helps: Reveals where attention leaks and where to reclaim it.

Reflection Questions

- In a current stress, what belongs to your inner, middle, and outer circles—and where are you spending most energy?
- When have you performed better after releasing outcome control and focusing on effort?
- Which friendships or online habits pull you into the outer circle most often, and what boundary will you set this week?
- Which virtue—wisdom, justice, courage, or temperance—would most improve your responses right now?
- What does "my part" look like today in school, at home, and online?

"Freedom begins the moment attention shifts from trying to control others to mastering one's own thoughts, choices, and actions."

Chapter 4: Taming the Emotional Storm

"No person is free who is not master of himself." — Epictetus

---

The Lightning-Rod Moment

Arjun paces the touchline, heat climbing his face, hands balled tight. He wants to launch his bottle into the sky, to drown the noise in his head: I blew it. Coach is done with me. The team can't trust me. His breath comes short and fast as the match resumes without him.

Lina, stretching a few steps away, catches the storm in his shoulders. "Want to breathe with me for a minute?" she asks, voice low. Arjun scowls, then nods once. They count ten slow breaths together. The ache remains, but the surge ebbs. He can hear words again, including the coach's clipped, useful feedback.

Nothing outside changed; a gap opened inside—space between impact and reaction.

The Space to Choose

Definition: Between an emotional surge and action lies assent—the decision to believe a thought or let it pass; freedom lives there.

Teen Example: The urge to clap back in a group chat isn't destiny; a pause makes room for a better reply—or none.

Why It Feels Like a Category Five

Arjun's afternoon class doesn't help; the highlight replay keeps ambushing him. His brain favors alarms over analysis today. That's normal. The body's alert system fires quickly; the planning center warms up slower. Rewards and embarrassment hit harder at his age, and a sideline can feel like a stage.

He remembers Lina's count and tries it again. Inhale four, exhale six. He labels what's happening: hot cheeks, tight chest, racing thoughts. Naming turns the storm into weather he can watch. The feeling is still strong; he doesn't have to do what it says.

First waves are automatic; the story told about them is optional.

First Movement vs. Passion

Definition: A first movement is an involuntary surge; passion is the runaway emotion that follows when we agree with a harsh judgment.

Teen Example: Blushing in class is automatic; deciding "I'm pathetic" is optional—and changeable.

Tools on the Sideline

At evening practice, Coach sets up penalty drills. Arjun's stomach flips. He imagines the goalbox shrinking. Then he tries a different sequence: pause, label, reframe, aim.

Pause: three slow breaths.
Label: fear in my gut, hands shaky.

Reframe: This is training, not a trial; discomfort means growth is happening.
Aim: pick the inside netting, head steady, plant foot firm.

He misses once, twice, then adjusts and drives the ball clean. The field doesn't erupt; a few teammates nod. The win is quieter than applause: he acted on a plan, not a panic.

Mastery grows when action follows values instead of mood.

Right Action Over Outcome
Definition: Measure success by what you can control—effort, focus, character—even when results vary.
Teen Example: A calm apology after snapping shows more strength than winning an argument.

Storms in Other Skies

Lina texts later about a different tempest—friend drama brewing online. They trade plans: mute, journal, move, sleep. Tomorrow they'll both face whatever shows up, practicing the same moves on new weather.

The day ends with a quick recap in Arjun's notebook: Trigger—missed kick. Judgment—"I'm done." Better story—"I missed; now I train." Next step—five set-piece reps after each practice this week. He closes the book lighter. The storm can return; the tools are packed.

Weather changes; practice continues.

The Inner Coach
Definition: A steady routine—breathing, perspective, reflection—builds a mental home that weather can't knock down.
Teen Example: Two minutes of morning intention and one page of night review add bricks to that home daily.

Practical Exercises

Six-Second Freeze — Breathe slowly for six seconds before replying or acting. Why it helps: Lets chemistry settle so judgment can lead.

Name It to Tame It — Say, "I'm feeling a surge of anger/shame/anxiety." Why it helps: Labels move the brain from reaction to observation.

The View from Above — Zoom out: field → school → city → planet. Why it helps: Shrinks intensity without denying reality.

Two-Step Reframe — Replace "This is a disaster" with "This is a challenge; my next step is _____." Why it helps: Swaps doom for direction.

Move the Body, Move the Mood — 90-second brisk walk, wall push-ups, or stairs. Why it helps: Burns off adrenaline; resets focus.

Reflection Questions

Think of your last emotional spike. Where did you intervene—at the surge, the story, or the action? Where could you step in next time?

Which practice—freeze, label, reframe, or zoom-out—fits you best under pressure, and how will you cue it?

What emotion visits most often lately? What useful message might it carry when you strip away exaggeration?

Choose one situation this week to measure by controllables only. What are they?

Build your 60-second "first-aid" kit: list three actions you will take the moment a surge hits.

"Emotions arrive like weather; freedom begins when a pause, a name, and a plan turn storms into training."

Chapter 5: Dealing with Anger and Frustration

"Anger, if not restrained, is frequently more hurtful to us than the injury that provokes it." — Seneca

---

The Smoldering Ember

Ravi's jaw locks as the wing snaps off his model. His brother's apology sounds far away. Heat climbs his chest, and the easiest option is volume—slam the door, spit the words, let the house feel what he feels. He grips the desk instead. Aarav, who was gaming on the floor, looks up. "Walk?" he asks, already slipping on sandals.

Outside, the first hundred steps are angry ones. Ravi's breath saws in and out. By the third block, the rhythm shifts. He can name what's happening: anger, embarrassment, a rush of unfairness. The plane is still broken. The world around him—buses, crows, a cricket shout from an alley—hasn't noticed.

Nothing external changed; a small internal lever did—pause before response.

Prosoché (Attentive Pause)

Definition: A conscious halt between surge and action creates space to choose a response that serves character, not impulse.

Teen Example: Before hitting "send," breathe twice and ask, "Will this message age well?"

Why Anger Feels Necessary

Back home, Ravi remembers other flare-ups—curfews, marks, sarcastic jokes that landed wrong. Anger often arrived dressed as justice. His body treated it like an emergency: tight jaw, fast heart, narrowed vision. The first surge felt useful, like fuel; the aftermath—guilt, cold silence, broken trust—never did.

He writes two columns on a sticky note: "What anger promises" and "What it delivers." Promises: power, protection, respect. Delivers: regret, more problems to fix, a tired mind. The mismatch is hard to ignore.

Feelings can be real and still be poor guides without a leader.

Discipline of Assent

Definition: Emotions present a story; reason decides whether to agree.

Teen Example: "He disrespected me" may be true—or it may be a guess; check the facts before you crown the thought.

Rewiring the Cycle

That evening, Ravi's brother peeks into the room with a glue tube and a guilty face. The surge returns—smaller, but present. Ravi tries a sequence he and Aarav practiced on the walk.

Freeze: six slow seconds.

Name: "Anger is here; I'm also sad about the work I lost."

Control check: I can't unbreak the wing. I can control my voice, the repair, the boundary.

Virtue cue: Justice (fairness to both), Temperance (self-control), Courage (saying what matters without heat).

He speaks evenly: "I'm upset. That plane took time. Help me fix it, and next time please ask before touching my stuff." They set parts on newspaper, watch a tutorial, and wait for the bond to set. It's not perfect. It's better than ashes.

Anger can become a signal light—warning, not steering.

Right Use of Emotion

Definition: Keep the part of anger that alerts you to values; remove the part that harms those values.

Teen Example: Channel "this matters" into a boundary, an apology request, or a plan—not into insults.

Tests Beyond the Bedroom

The next day offers new sparks: a group project freeloader, a referee's missed call, a parent's "Not now." Ravi doesn't win every round. He does win more pauses. He drafts a firm message to his group with clear tasks and a deadline. He jogs off frustration after the match instead of arguing. He waits ten minutes and asks his parent again with specifics.

At night, he journals in three lines: Trigger—broken plane. Default impulse—shout, slam. Better path—pause, boundary, repair. He circles one word for tomorrow: "Steady."

Patience isn't passive; it's directed strength applied over time.

Patience as Strength

Definition: Patience is anger domesticated—energy held steady until it can do good work.

Teen Example: Training quietly every day for a spot is harder—and more powerful—than starting a fight about playing time.

Practical Toolkit: Daily Anger Mastery

Six-Second Rule — Inhale 4, exhale 6 before words leave your mouth. Why it helps: Lets the body downshift so the mind can steer.

Name + Frame — "Anger is present; my value here is _____." Why it helps: Converts raw heat into a value-aligned aim.

Boundary Script — "When X happens, I feel Y. I need Z next time." Why it helps: Sets clear, respectful expectations without blame.

Move It Out — 90-second brisk walk, wall push-ups, or skipping rope. Why it helps: Burns adrenaline, reduces shaking and tunnel vision.

Repair Ritual — If anger spills, own it fast: "I spoke harshly. I'm sorry. Here's my plan to fix it." Why it helps: Restores trust and self-respect.

Special Case Files

A) Family Frustrations — Assume positive intent unless proven otherwise; schedule the talk, don't spring it mid-heat. Bring one request, not ten.

B) Peer Conflicts — Seek dignity for both sides. Offer a path forward ("Can we reset this?") rather than a courtroom.

C) Self-Directed Anger — Swap "I am a failure" for "I failed at X today." Turn blame into a plan with time blocks and help requests.

Reflection Questions

In your last flare-up, where did you lose control—surge, story, or speech? What would a six-second win have looked like?

Which virtue—wisdom, justice, courage, or temperance—would most improve your responses this week?

What boundary do you need to state calmly in one sentence? Write it now.

How can you convert your top anger trigger into a training plan (skill, script, or schedule)?

When you slip, what is your two-line repair?

"Anger is energy—use the pause to aim it with virtue, and it becomes patience that builds, not fire that burns."

Chapter 6: Overcoming Fear and Anxiety

"He is a wise man who does not grieve for the things which he has not, but rejoices for those which he has." — Epictetus

---

The Shadow in the Mind

Anaya stands backstage, palms damp, throat tight. The auditorium hums. Her thoughts crowd the doorway: What if I freeze? What if they laugh? The fear feels like a shadow that knows all her weak spots. She pinches the note card, breathes in for four counts, out for six, and focuses on the first line only. Not the whole speech—just the first clear step.

Across campus, Kabir crowds at a computer terminal, refreshing the results portal. His mind sprints through futures he can't yet live: a rejection email, disappointed faces at dinner, dreams collapsing in one click. He sits back, shuts his eyes, and asks a quieter question: What can I do with the next ten minutes? He opens a blank doc and outlines a backup plan, then a plan if the news is good. The portal will open when it opens. His choices can start now.

Fear multiplies in imagined futures; it shrinks in the present step taken well.

Present Control

Definition: Anxiety lives in tomorrow's "what-ifs"; strength grows by acting on what can be chosen now—breath, words, posture, next task.

Teen Example: Before a speech, rehearse the first sentence and where to look; let the rest follow.

Why Fear Feels Bigger Than You

Anaya's heart thuds because her body is doing its job—prepping for challenge. The brain's alarm rings fast; the planning center answers slower. That doesn't mean danger; it means energy. She names what's happening: fast pulse, warm hands, narrow focus. Naming changes the weather from storm to forecast. She isn't her fear; she's a person noticing fear.

Kabir sketches three circles on a scrap: inner—effort, attitude, next study block; middle—how clearly he asks teachers for feedback; outer—final cutoffs, committee moods. The third circle is loud but not his. He circles the first and sets a 20-minute timer for quiet work while he waits.

The body speaks in signals; judgment decides the meaning.

First Signals vs. Story

Definition: Physical surges are natural "first movements"; suffering grows when we add catastrophic stories.

Teen Example: Sweaty hands before tryouts mean readiness, not failure—channel the energy into the warm-up.

Training Courage in Small Steps

Anaya steps onto the stage, not fear-free, but with a micro-plan: plant feet, look at the third row, speak the first sentence, pause, breathe, continue. She rides wave by wave. A stumble arrives; she smiles and keeps going. The room softens with her. Afterward, a younger student thanks her for the line about "trying scared."

Kabir's results arrive after lunch. The dream school says no. His chest drops; the sting is real. He allows five minutes to feel it, then opens the plan he made during the wait. He messages a counselor, drafts a new essay for his next choice, and texts a friend to walk after school. Fear said rejection would end him. It didn't. It redirected him.

Courage is built by doing the next right thing with shaky hands.

Courage as Repetition

Definition: Courage grows like a muscle—through repeated, small acts done despite fear.

Teen Example: Speak once in class today; tomorrow, ask the follow-up.

Reframing the Unknown

That evening, Anaya writes down three "worst cases" for an upcoming debate and answers each with a clear response: If I forget a point, I paraphrase and move on. If someone laughs, I keep my pace and finish the sentence. If I blank, I pause, breathe, and read my note card. Seeing the map shrinks the monster.

Kabir lists what remains: friends who care, teachers willing to help, his work ethic, his curiosity. He doesn't pretend the "no" is good news. He does refuse to let it define his worth or his future. Fear loses leverage when gratitude picks up the other side of the bar.

The future is large; so is the toolkit you can carry into it.

Negative Visualization

Definition: Briefly imagine setbacks to rehearse wise responses and drain dread of surprise.

Teen Example: Picture missing a bus; plan the text, the alternate route, and how to stay calm.

Practical Toolkit: Daily Courage and Calm

4-6 Breathing — Inhale 4, exhale 6 for 2 minutes. Why it helps: Calms the nervous system so focus returns.

Two-Sentence Anchor — Memorize the opening two lines of a talk or conversation. Why it helps: Lowers startup anxiety and builds momentum.

Fear Audit — Write "What I fear," then "Evidence for/against," then "My next step." Why it helps: Replaces vague dread with a plan.

Exposure Ladder — Break a fear into five rungs from easy to hard; climb one rung per day. Why it helps: Gradual wins teach the brain safety.

Evening Wins Log — Note three actions taken despite discomfort. Why it helps: Trains identity toward "I'm someone who acts."

Special Case Files

A) Fear of Failure — Treat outcomes as feedback loops. After any test/game/audition: three strengths, two gaps, one adjustment.

B) Social Anxiety — Prepare a simple script: greeting, one question, one comment. Enter, stay two minutes, exit kindly.

C) Fear of the Future — Set a 25-minute "future block" for applications/research; close with a five-minute gratitude list to balance the mind.

Reflection Questions

Which "what-ifs" visit most often, and which belong to the outer circle of control?

What is today's "tiny brave" step, and when will it happen?

Which story most often inflates your fear, and what balanced story will replace it?

After your last fear moment, what did you learn that could become a routine?

Who can be your "stage buddy" or "waiting buddy" to practice breathing and perspective together?

"Fear shrinks when attention returns to the present step—breathe, choose, act—and grows smaller each time courage shows up to walk beside it."

Chapter 7: The Four Pillars of Strength

"If a man knows not to which port he sails, no wind is favorable."
— Seneca
"Waste no more time arguing about what a good man should be. Be one."
— Marcus Aurelius

The Foundation Beneath the Storm

Rohan sits on the bleachers after practice, phone buzzing with college reminders, a family chat flaring about money, and whispers about last night's party. Each ping asks him to be someone different. His coach sits beside him. "Pressure doesn't build character—it reveals it. Know what you stand on." The words land heavier than the cleats in Rohan's bag. If he doesn't choose a foundation, the noise will choose one for him.

The Stoics called that foundation the virtues—habits of excellence no crisis can take away.

Virtue as Foundation

Definition: Virtues are stable inner standards that guide choices when circumstances shake.

Teen Example: Grades can rise and fall; honesty doesn't have to.

Why Virtues Beat Goals

On the bus home, Rohan lists goals: cut-off scores, starting spot, internship. Every one depends on someone else's "yes." Then he lists virtues: clear judgment, fairness, bravery, self-control. No committee can grant or revoke those. He realizes goals set direction, but virtues decide how he travels—and who he becomes on the way.

Meet the four pillars that steady a life in motion.

Port Before Wind

Definition: If you don't know your moral destination, speed only gets you lost faster.

Teen Example: A full timetable doesn't help if it steers away from the person you want to be.

Pillars at Work

That week tests him. A friend DMs leaked answers before a math test. Wisdom asks, "True? Necessary? Aligned?" He studies instead. In the cafeteria, a new student gets edged out of a table. Justice nudges him to make space and introduce names. Debate tryouts open; his stomach flips. Courage says, "Speak once. Then again tomorrow." That night, a group chat drags past midnight. Temperance walks the phone to the other side of the room and sets an alarm. None of these moments are dramatic. Together, they feel like bricks under his feet.

The pillars aren't theories; they're practiced in small choices that add up to who a person is.

Character by Repetition

Definition: Identity forms through repeated actions aligned with values.

Teen Example: Five honest study sessions build "I'm the kind of person who…," more than one lucky score ever could.

When One Pillar Wobbles

Friday brings a stumble. Rohan snaps at a sibling, then scrolls too long, then mails a sloppy draft. He sees the wobble clearly—temperance slipped, wisdom followed. Instead of spiraling, he repairs: apology, timer, revision. A pillar can crack and still be strengthened. The point isn't perfection; it's return.

Virtues reinforce each other—strengthening one often steadies the rest.

Mutual Support

Definition: Wisdom chooses well; justice checks impact; courage follows through; temperance keeps balance.

Teen Example: Saying the right thing kindly at the right time takes all four.

Practical Exercises

1) Daily Pillar Focus — Choose one virtue each morning and write one action that will embody it today. Why it helps: Narrow targets turn ideals into behavior.

2) Three-Filter Test (Wisdom) — True? Necessary? Aligned? Why it helps: Cuts rumor, rush, and regret before they start.

3) Justice Check-in — Ask, "Who is helped or harmed by this choice?" Why it helps: Keeps relationships and reputation strong.

4) Tiny Brave (Courage) — Do one small fearful thing before noon: ask, apply, speak. Why it helps: Courage grows through reps, not pep talks.

5) Pause Button (Temperance) — Move the phone away; set a 25-minute timer; stop at "enough." Why it helps: Protects attention and sleep so judgment and grit recover.

Reflection Questions

- Which pillar feels most natural to you right now, and which buckles under pressure? Why?
- Think of a recent decision. How would it change if wisdom, justice, courage, and temperance each had a vote?
- What one daily habit would most strengthen your weakest pillar this week?
- When did someone your age show a quiet act of justice or courage that changed a room?
- How might living by these pillars alter how you handle exams, team dynamics, and family stress over the next year?

"Choose pillars first—wisdom, justice, courage, temperance—and let every goal, habit, and relationship rest on the steadiness they provide."

Chapter 8: Developing Self-Discipline

"No man is free who is not master of himself." — Epictetus

The Battle Within

Aria sits at her desk beneath a small mountain of books. The room is quiet; her screen is not. A new reel flashes, a message pings, a notification glows like an invitation to anywhere but here. Tomorrow's exam grows larger in her mind while the study hour shrinks. She hears the bargain her brain keeps offering: five more minutes, and then I'll start. She knows that promise. It never keeps itself.

She flips her phone, face down, and the urge rises hotter. The tug isn't just habit; it's chemistry. She closes her eyes and counts a slow breath in, a slower breath out. "What kind of person do I want to be—right now?" The question lands like a weight that steadies rather than crushes. She opens her notebook and writes the first heading.

Self-discipline begins where urges end and identity starts—at the moment of choice.

Prosoché (Attentive Focus)

Definition: Direct, deliberate attention to the present task interrupts impulse and puts reason back in charge.

Teen Example: Before opening an app, ask, "Why am I here, and for how long?"

Why It Feels So Hard

Later that evening, Aria notices the pattern. The phone promises quick reward; the chapter offers slow progress. Her brain prefers the spark to the steady flame. Decision after decision drains energy until "later" becomes default. She isn't weak; she's human—and the environment is engineered to win.

She sketches a simple map: triggers (boredom, stress, late-night fatigue), default responses (scroll, snack, stall), better options (timer, water, stretch, one tiny step). Seeing the loops on paper makes them less mysterious, more manageable. Discipline, she realizes, is not one giant refusal; it's many small re-directions.

Systems beat willpower—especially when the system starts before the temptation.

Premeditatio (Planning Ahead)

Definition: Anticipate likely obstacles and set responses in advance so emotion doesn't set the plan for you.

Teen Example: Put the phone in another room before starting a study block.

Turning Toward the Work

Aria sets a 25-minute timer and chooses the tiniest possible start: five definitions. The first minutes drag; the middle settles; the last five feel almost smooth. When the timer chimes, she stands, drinks water, and moves for a minute. A second round follows more easily. Momentum grows not from motivation but from motion.

Messages pile up without her. She doesn't punish herself for wanting them; she just defers them. One hour becomes two focused blocks. When she finally checks her phone, the pull is still there—but softer. She answers what matters and leaves the rest.

Progress is a practice, not a mood—show up small, then keep showing up.

Right Action Over Feeling

Definition: Do the next right thing regardless of whether enthusiasm is present; feelings can follow.

Teen Example: Start the assignment for two minutes—often the mind warms to the work once begun.

After the Slip

The next night, Aria stumbles. A late message turns into a long scroll; the study plan collapses. Shame knocks, ready to turn one miss into a story about failure. She chooses a different story: review, repair, recommit. She logs what triggered the slide, sets a firmer boundary for tomorrow, and sleeps on time. Self-discipline grows not by never slipping, but by returning faster, kinder, clearer.

The disciplined person is not the one who never falls—it's the one who rises with a plan.

The Inner Citadel

Definition: A simple daily routine—intention, effort, review—builds a resilient center that distractions can't easily breach.

Teen Example: Two minutes to set a morning aim; two minutes to reflect at night—every day.

Practical Exercises

1) Two-Minute Doorway — Begin with 2 minutes of the task, no excuses. Why it helps: Defeats inertia; small starts unlock bigger work.

2) 25–5 Focus Cycles — Work 25 minutes, break 5; repeat 3–4 times. Why

it helps: Preserves energy and combats decision fatigue.

3) Phone Far, Not Near — Keep the phone in another room during blocks. Why it helps: Removes frictionless temptation so attention stays local.

4) If-Then Plans — "If I feel the urge to scroll, then I'll stand, sip water, and do one example." Why it helps: Preloads wise responses for hot moments.

5) Night Review, Next Cue — Write one sentence: "Tomorrow at 7:30, I will start with Chapter 3 Q1–5." Why it helps: Turns goals into appointments the brain can keep.

Reflection Questions

- What are the top three triggers that pull attention off course? What preplanned responses will you use for each?
- Which controllable action, done daily, would most improve your week?
- Where did you slip recently, and how can you design the environment so the wiser choice is easier next time?
- Which virtue—wisdom, justice, courage, or temperance—would most strengthen your self-discipline today?
- What tiny, repeatable start can you commit to for the next five days?

"Self-discipline is the freedom to act by choice, not impulse—built through small, repeated decisions that align attention with values."

Chapter 9: The Art of Patience

"The whole future lies in uncertainty: live immediately." — Seneca

---

The Waiting Game

Kavya traces raindrops on the window while thunder rolls in the distance. The scholarship results were "coming soon" two weeks ago. Each quiet hour feels louder than the last. Thoughts crowd in: What if I'm not good enough? What if this was my only chance? Her stomach knots, fingers drum the sill, and refreshing the inbox becomes a reflex.

Her cousin sits beside her, not to fix anything, but to sit through the noise. "Patience isn't waiting," she says softly. "It's what you do while you wait." The sentence lands like a small anchor. Kavya realizes she's spent days staring at a door she can't open yet—and ignoring the rooms she can still move in.

When the future won't answer, wisdom calls attention back to the present—where choices still live.

Present Action

Definition: Patience directs energy to what can be done now rather than clinging to outcomes that aren't here yet.

Teen Example: While results are pending, refine the next application, rehearse the audition piece, or strengthen a study habit.

Why Patience Feels So Hard

The next morning she notices the tug-of-war. Part of her craves control; another part knows some things won't budge. Add a brain that loves quick feedback and a culture that delivers instant everything, and waiting feels like failure. It isn't. It's training.

Kavya sketches a simple cycle in her notebook: anticipation → frustration → urgency to force → exhaustion → regret. Then she draws a second loop: anticipation → pause → present task → small progress → steadier mood. The first loop drains; the second builds.

Patience isn't passive—it's a practiced sequence that replaces urgency with useful steps.

Prosoché (Attentive Presence)

Definition: A deliberate pause resets attention, interrupts impatience, and restores choice.

Teen Example: Before refreshing your inbox again, take six slow breaths and do two minutes of the next right task.

The Practice of Waiting Well

She makes a plan: mornings for scholarship essays she can still improve, afternoons for schoolwork, evenings for a brisk walk and one chapter of a novel that calms her mind. When restlessness spikes, she labels it and moves her body—stairs, stretches, a glass of water.

Midweek, a friend texts a rumor about decisions dropping that night. The urge to camp by the phone surges. Kavya tries the six-second pause, then asks, "What's in my hands?" She schedules a 20-minute window to check at 8 p.m., then returns to the paragraph she's revising. The rumor fizzles. Her progress doesn't.

Patience grows by rhythms and boundaries—time blocks for checking, longer blocks for living.

Dichotomy of Control

Definition: Aim effort at what you command (attention, preparation, routine) and accept what you don't (timelines, decisions).

Teen Example: Set two check-in times per day; spend the rest building skills that matter regardless of the result.

When the News Finally Comes

The email arrives late Friday. It's not the answer she wanted. Her chest drops. She lets the sadness be real. Then, following her plan, she walks, journals three lines—what hurts, what matters, what's next—and opens the list of alternate scholarships she prepared. The rejection still stings; it doesn't steer.

A week later, she notices something surprising: the habits built during waiting—steady work, calmer evenings, planned check-ins—still hold. Patience didn't just help her wait. It changed how she moves through time.

Outcomes end; patience remains. It's a skill that outlives every decision email.

The Obstacle Becomes the Way

Definition: Delays can train resilience, focus, and creativity—qualities more valuable than speed.

Teen Example: A postponed tryout becomes extra practice time; a delayed reply becomes a chance to draft a better message.

Practical Exercises

1) Six-Second Pause — Breathe slowly for six seconds when restlessness spikes. Why it helps: Lowers urgency so judgment can lead.

2) Two Check Windows — Choose exact times to look for updates (e.g., 8 a.m., 8 p.m.). Why it helps: Containment stops compulsive refreshing.

3) Wait-Well List — Keep a list of small, meaningful tasks for waiting

periods. Why it helps: Converts dead time into progress.

4) Negative Visualization — Briefly imagine delay or "no," then outline your response. Why it helps: Drains dread and prepares action.

5) Evening "Three Lines" — Write: What tested me? How I responded? One improvement tomorrow. Why it helps: Turns waiting into training data.

Reflection Questions

- What are you currently waiting for, and which parts are in your control versus outside it?
- Which thought most inflames your impatience? What truer, kinder thought could replace it?
- How will you design two daily windows to check for updates—and what will you do between them?
- Which virtue (wisdom, justice, courage, temperance) would most improve your waiting this week, and what's one action to practice it?
- When has a delay in your life secretly helped you—by improving your work, deepening relationships, or strengthening resolve?

"Patience is active endurance—focus on what you can do now, and let time do what only time can do."

CHAPTER 10: FRIENDS, FRENEMIES, AND TOXIC PEOPLE

"The best way to take care of the future is to take care of the present moment." — Thich Nhat Hanh

"Associate with people who are likely to improve you." — Seneca

---

The Invisible Battlefield

Priya sets her tray on the cafeteria table and freezes. Laughter rolls across the plates, but the words sting: casual jokes at Meera's expense, "helpful" critiques that aren't kind, a chorus of approval. Kavya's eyes meet hers—uneasy, asking a question without sound. Priya stands on a thin edge: sit and blend in, say nothing and feel smaller, or step toward the person she wants to be.

Her palms dampen. She thinks about last week, when Meera practiced debate notes with them, hopeful and brave. Silence would be easy. It would also be expensive—paid for with self-respect. Priya draws a breath.

Friendship choices are character choices in disguise.

Company Shapes Character

Definition: We become like those we spend time with—so choose companions who call out the best, not the worst.

Teen Example: Hang with people who study, include others, and own mistakes; their habits will rub off.

The Spectrum of Connection

At practice later, Priya replays the moment. Not all friendships are equal. Some feel like sun—warmth and growth. Some are weather—fine until storms. Some are smoke—hard to breathe, hard to see clearly. She can name them now: true friends, fair-weather friends, frenemies, and the truly toxic. The labels aren't for judging people, she decides, but for choosing wisely.

She remembers Seneca's advice about choosing companions who improve us. Improvement isn't flattery; it's honesty paired with care. She writes a quick list in her notes app: who helps me grow, who drains me, where I enable harm.

Clarity precedes courage; once the map is drawn, the path appears.

The Virtue Test

Definition: Measure friendships by whether they nudge you toward wisdom, justice, courage, and temperance.

Teen Example: Does this group make it easier or harder to be kind when it's unpopular?

Boundaries and Better Roads

The next day, Priya arrives early and sits with Kavya. "That didn't feel right," she says. Relief crosses Kavya's face. Together they plan simple, friendly lines for the next time gossip starts: "Let's not drag her—how's your tryout going?" or "If she wants debate, we can help her prep." Small sentences can shift a table.

When the moment comes, Aisha starts again. Priya answers lightly but firmly, then changes the subject. It's not a speech; it's a nudge. The laughter dulls. Dev shrugs and moves on. Later, Priya texts Meera to practice after school. The invitation costs her nothing and buys back a lot.

Boundaries are bridges—they protect values and offer a better way forward.

Gentle Resistance

Definition: Say no to harmful talk without hostility, and offer an alternative everyone can take.

Teen Example: "Let's not; she's not here. Tell me about your game instead."

When Distance Is the Right Choice

Not every circle shifts. Some double down. Over the next weeks, Priya sees patterns: certain jokes keep cutting; a friend's "advice" often hides competition. She doesn't stage a breakup. She reallocates time—more with people who build, less where she shrinks. The cafeteria feels different now: fewer laughs at others' expense, more real conversations, a little more quiet, a lot more peace.

One afternoon, Meera speaks at the debate showcase. She's nervous, then steady, then good. Priya claps hard. She isn't trying to fix the whole school. She's changing a corner of it—starting with her own table.

Influence grows when integrity leads; even small circles can ripple far.

Inner Citadel, Social Edition

Definition: Hold to your values in any crowd; let behavior match principles, not pressure.

Teen Example: If friends push a boundary, keep yours—and invite them to meet you there.

Practical Exercises

1) Circle Map — List close contacts and note "builds," "neutral," or "drains." Why it helps: Clarifies where to invest time and where to set limits.
2) Three Redirects — Prepare three kind topic shifts for gossip moments. Why it helps: Reduces freeze time and keeps tone friendly.
3) Boundary Script — Write one sentence for a repeated issue ("I'm not okay with trashing people."). Why it helps: Clear, rehearsed lines lower anxiety.
4) Friendship Minimums — Define basics you require (respect, honesty, support). Why it helps: Prevents slow compromises.
5) Weekly Ally Act — Do one concrete thing that lifts someone (invite, include, encourage). Why it helps: Builds the culture you want to live in.

Reflection Questions

- Which relationships leave you more honest, brave, fair, and balanced—and which pull you away from those?
- When did you last redirect a harmful conversation or wish you had? What line will you use next time?
- Where do you need a boundary—and what single sentence will state it simply?
- What small change to your social time would shift you toward healthier circles this month?
- How can you be a better friend this week while still protecting your values?

"Choose companions who help you practice your values; when talk turns harmful, lead with a kind boundary—and, if needed, walk toward better tables."

Chapter 11: Family Dynamics and Independence

"The happiness of your life depends upon the quality of your thoughts."
- Marcus Aurelius

The Changing Tides of Home

Aarav sits at the kitchen table while the evening hum gathers—pressure-cooked rice hissing, his sister's headphones leaking a beat, his parents speaking in calm voices that carry worry. Curfew, grades, money, timing—threads that keep knotting. Yesterday's attempt at a later curfew ended with, "You're not ready." The words sting because part of him believes he is.

He notices two pulls: the door promising space and the home asking for steadiness. He wants both. The old way—argue hard, withdraw harder—never worked. He opens his notes app and writes: What's mine to steer? What's theirs? The questions cool his face.

Independence begins by sorting control—what to shape inside, what to accept outside.

Dichotomy of Control (at home)

Definition: You don't control your parents' fears or rules; you do control your attitude, effort, reliability, and the way you ask for change.

Teen Example: You can't force a later curfew tonight; you can build a track record that earns it next month.

Independence Through Responsibility

The next week, Aarav tries a different approach. He lists the responsibilities he can own without reminders—house chores, study blocks, texting location when late, returning on time. He shares the list before asking for anything. "I'll do these for three weeks. If I keep it, can we try curfew at 10:30 on Fridays with check-ins?"

His parents trade a look. The request lands differently - less demand, more partnership. The trial period begins. Some nights are easy; some are tired and tempting. He chooses the message before the match, the sink before the screen. Trust doesn't leap; it grows.

Freedom expands where proof piles up - small, consistent acts that say "I'm ready."

Virtue Signals

Definition: Wisdom, justice, courage, and temperance are best argued by behavior, not speeches.
Teen Example: Returning five minutes early says more than five paragraphs ever will.

The Art of Respectful Talk

Conflict still visits. One night, a plan changes and everyone is tired. Aarav tries a new script: "I want to understand your concern first." He listens fully, repeats back the point, then shares his view: "Here's how I'm planning to keep it safe." When voices rise, he uses the six-second pause, then asks to finish later. Later comes, and the tone is better.

He learns that being heard often requires hearing first. He doesn't win every request. He does win the room more often—less heat, more clarity, fewer old patterns dragging them around.

Respectful communication turns standoffs into problem-solving.

Discipline of Assent (in conversations)

Definition: Don't sign every hot thought; pause, check for accuracy, and then speak your best words.

Teen Example: Replace "You never trust me" with "Here's what I've done to earn trust, and here's what I'm asking next."

Balance: Autonomy and Belonging

On Saturday, the family budget talk returns. Worry lives under the numbers. Aarav notices the urge to escape and chooses contribution instead—pulls up scholarship links, offers to take on a weekend tutoring gig, cooks dal while his sister sets the table. The room softens.

Later that night, he walks with a friend who is ready to fight at home for more freedom. Aarav shares what's working: show up, own your part, ask with a plan, accept a trial. The door to independence opens wider—not by pushing against family, but by pulling with them.

Interdependence doesn't shrink freedom; it supports it.

Inner Citadel (family edition)

Definition: A calm, value-led routine—intention, effort, review—keeps you steady in family storms.

Teen Example: Morning aim: "Respect and patience." Evening review: one win, one repair.

Practical Exercises

1) Responsibility Ledger — Write and track 3–5 home responsibilities for 21 days. Why it helps: Visible reliability builds trust faster than promises.
2) Trial-Term Ask — Propose a time-limited privilege tied to clear conditions. Why it helps: Reduces risk for parents; increases chances of "yes."
3) Six-Second Pause — Breathe before responding when voices rise. Why it helps: Prevents escalation; keeps conversations recoverable.
4) Perspective Swap — Summarize your parent's concern before sharing yours. Why it helps: Being heard begins with hearing.
5) Family Gratitude Ping — One sentence daily appreciating a family member's effort. Why it helps: Shifts tone from defense to partnership.

Reflection Questions

- Where do family expectations feel tightest, and which parts are truly under your control?
- What responsibilities, if handled flawlessly for three weeks, would most strengthen trust?
- How does your tone change outcomes at home? What sentence starter will you try next time?
- Which virtue—wisdom, justice, courage, or temperance—would most improve your family life this week? What's one action to practice it?
- Think of a recent conflict. How would the six-second pause and "SAY" script have changed it?

"Independence grows from responsibility—bring proof, speak with respect, accept what you can't command, and freedom follows."

CHAPTER 12: LOVE, DATING, AND HEARTBREAK

"He who is not a master of himself will always be a slave."
-Epictetus
"When we kiss, we want it to be forever. But life wants us to learn."
- Adaptation of a Stoic sentiment

The Highs and Lows of Young Love

Rhea sits in the corner booth where Friday evenings used to feel endless. The seat across from her is empty; the cappuccino cools untouched. A month ago this table was a small galaxy—shared jokes, warm hands, plans that reached years ahead. Now the words she didn't expect loop in her mind: I just don't feel the same anymore.

The world keeps moving beyond the window—buses, umbrellas, rush. Inside, time slows. What if I had tried harder? What if this was it? The thoughts pile up until the room feels smaller than her chest. She wants the story back. She also wants to feel like herself again.

Love can be beautiful and blinding; Stoic clarity helps the heart breathe when the story changes.

Dichotomy of Control (in love)

Definition: Feelings and outcomes aren't fully ours; honesty, kindness, and how we respond always are.

Teen Example: A partner's interest may fade; dignity and respectful closure are choices that remain.

Why It Feels So Intense

Rhea remembers the early weeks—every message a spark, every plan a promise. Her brain loved the rush; perspective took a back seat. Music, reels, and friends' highlight stories all whispered the same script: if it's real, it's forever; if it ends, it must mean you failed. The script made ordinary disagreements sound like alarms.

Identity tangled with romance quickly—his praise felt like proof she mattered; his silence felt like a verdict. First love stamped the memory extra deep, setting a standard no one could keep. Seeing this clearly doesn't make the pain vanish. It makes it honest.

Naming the forces—chemistry, culture, identity—shrinks the monster and returns agency.

Discipline of Assent

Definition: A painful thought is not a fact; pause and test it before believing.
Teen Example: "I'm unlovable" becomes "I am hurting; my worth isn't on trial."

Weathering Heartbreak Well

The first nights are hardest. Rhea lets the tears come, sets screen limits, and asks two close friends for company without the autopsy of every text. She writes three columns: what was good, what was true but hard, what she'll do differently next time. The list isn't about blame; it's about learning.

She practices small rituals: a walk after school, fifteen minutes of guitar, one page of journaling. When the urge to message him surges, she uses a six-second breath, then asks, Is this aligned with my healing? Sometimes the answer is no; sometimes it's write but don't send. Gradually, the day includes more than the loss.

Healing is a sequence—feel, pause, choose, repeat—guided by values, not impulses.

The Inner Citadel (after a breakup)
Definition: Simple routines—sleep, movement, reflection—protect a steady center while feelings rise and fall.
Teen Example: Morning intention, afternoon walk, night journal; repeat until the heart catches up.

Love with Wisdom

Weeks later, Rhea meets a friend for coffee in the same café. It still echoes, but less loudly. She realizes she can cherish what was and wish him well without clinging. Next time—whenever it comes—she wants to keep parts of herself independent: music, friends, studies, the quiet space that belongs only to her. She doesn't want a half-life inside a relationship or a hollow life without one.

She smiles at a simple truth: love is best when it's two whole people walking side by side. If paths diverge, character gets the last word.

The aim isn't to love less; it's to love wisely—fully, freely, and without losing yourself.

Virtue Filter (for choices in love)

Definition: Act in ways that reflect wisdom, justice, courage, and temperance—especially at the beginning and the end.
Teen Example: Be honest about feelings early; end with clarity and kindness if they change.

Practical Exercises
1) Love's Ledger — Write three lists: what was good, what was hard, what I learned. Why it helps: Turns rumination into wisdom.
2) Two-Week Cooldown — Limit contact and social media checks post-breakup. Why it helps: Reduces re-injury so healing can begin.
3) Gratitude + Growth — Each night, one gratitude not about romance, one small growth action for tomorrow. Why it helps: Rebuilds identity beyond the relationship.

4) Virtue Rehearsal — Before a tough conversation, speak your lines once with wisdom, once with justice, once with courage, once with temperance. Why it helps: Aligns words with values, not panic.
5) Boundary Script — "I care about you and myself. For now I need space/no late-night texts." Why it helps: Protects healing without hostility.

Reflection Questions
- What parts of a relationship are truly within your control, and which never were?
- How have cultural scripts shaped your expectations about "forever" and "failure" in love?
- Which virtue do you most need to practice in your current situation—wisdom, justice, courage, or temperance?
- After a past heartbreak, what strengths did you gain that you still carry?
- If this relationship ended tomorrow, what would you want to remember about how you behaved?

"Love fully and act by virtue; when endings come, let character—not impulse—write the final scene."

Chapter 13: When Life Gets Hard

"Fire tests gold, adversity tests the brave." — Seneca
"The obstacle is the way." — Marcus Aurelius

A Day That Changes Everything

The calls arrive mid-practice. Ishaan's mother never interrupts drills, which is how he knows before he knows. Twenty minutes later he's racing past the pharmacy and the tea stall, watching his neighborhood blur into something unfamiliar. The living room smells like worry. ICU. Stroke. Words that are bigger than his age.

The week folds into corridors, vending-machine coffee, and forms he doesn't understand. His father, who shouted encouragement at every game, lies quiet beneath machines that beep like distant metronomes. Homework seems small. So does laughter. Questions don't stop: Why us? Will he wake? What happens now?

When life tilts, the first task isn't to solve the future; it's to find a steady place to stand.

Present-Moment Anchor

Definition: In chaos, shrink the horizon to the next clear step—one hour, one call, one task.

Teen Example: While waiting on updates, text your teacher you'll need an extension and pack a snack for a long hospital visit.

Why The First Storm Hits So Hard

Ishaan discovers a new kind of tired—the kind that comes from fear. Teen life rarely trains for this: the first big loss, the first time home stops feeling safe, the first proof that adults aren't invincible. His mind jumps weeks ahead; his body wants to curl into now. Both are understandable. Neither helps by itself.

He tries a small ritual: three slow breaths before each decision. What's mine? What isn't? That question doesn't fix anything. It does sort the mess into piles he can touch and piles he cannot.

Control isn't power over outcomes; it's mastery over responses.

Dichotomy of Control (in crisis)

Definition: Put energy only where your actions matter; accept what falls outside your hands without giving up.

Teen Example: You can't change test dates today, but you can email your counselor and ask for a plan.

The Way Through Is Through

Days stack. Ishaan starts running early—ten quiet minutes before the house wakes. He makes tea for his mother without being asked. He keeps a note on his phone labeled "Questions for the doctor" because memory isn't reliable when stress is loud. After school, he visits the ICU, studies one hour, sleeps on time. Not a perfect day—a survival day with intention.

When fear spikes, he imagines meeting it like a sparring partner: not to win in one blow, but to keep his feet and learn its moves. He hears Marcus: what blocks you can become the work. The obstacle is the way—one steady step after another.

Resilience is built from routine, not from rare heroics.

The Inner Citadel (under pressure)

Definition: Small daily structures—movement, nourishment, reflection—protect judgment when emotions run high.

Teen Example: Keep a two-line journal: "What hit me today? How did I respond?"

Turning Pain Into Purpose

Weeks pass. His father squeezes a hand. Progress is slow. Bills still exist; so do classes. Ishaan tutors a younger teammate for pocket money, starts a fundraiser page with a trusted adult, and accepts friends' offers to bring dinner twice a week. He stops pretending he's fine and starts saying, "Here's how you can help."

On the court, he plays fewer minutes but with clearer eyes. Every drill feels like practice for something larger—breathing when winded, choosing the next right pass, trusting a team. The storm hasn't ended; he's learning to sail in it.

Meaning doesn't erase pain; it gives pain a place to go.

Purpose as Anchor

Definition: Serving others and pursuing what remains within reach stabilizes the mind in hardship.

Teen Example: Help with siblings' homework, organize hospital rides, or keep one personal goal alive.

Practical Exercises

1) Next-Hour Plan — Write three tiny actions for the next 60 minutes. Why it helps: Shrinks overwhelm into doable steps.

2) Two-List Sort — "Mine / Not Mine" before big worries. Why it helps:

Redirects energy from rumination to action.

3) Voluntary Discomfort — Cold shower, device-free commute, or simple meals once a week. Why it helps: Trains the mind to stay calm when comfort drops.

4) Negative Visualization — Briefly picture a setback and rehearse your response. Why it helps: Reduces shock and speeds skillful action.

5) Purpose Ping — Do one helpful act daily (message, chore, errand). Why it helps: Service interrupts spirals and builds meaning.

Special Case Files

A) Illness in the Family — Show up reliably: small chores, calm updates, patient listening. Ask medical staff questions at set times; avoid constant hovering.

B) Academic Setbacks — Treat a failed exam as a diagnostic, not a verdict: three strengths, two gaps, one adjustment. Schedule office hours; change methods, not just hours.

C) Social Loss or Betrayal — Keep dignity. Don't feed drama. Invest in neutral spaces (clubs, teams) where new connections grow.

D) Financial Shock / Moving — Anchor to portable habits: wake time, study block, movement, gratitude. Carry your values; places will change.

Reflection Questions

- Recall a hard season. Which virtue—wisdom, justice, courage, temperance—helped most? Which was missing?
- What are your top three controllables this week—and what big worries belong in the "not mine" pile?
- Which simple routine (sleep, study block, walk, journal) would steady you most right now?
- Who models resilience in your life? What single habit of theirs can you copy this month?
- How can you turn a current difficulty into a source of service or learning?

"Adversity is unavoidable; agency is not—focus on the next right step, practice the virtues, and let the storm make you strong."

Chapter 14: The Pressure to Succeed

"It is not that we have a short time to live, but that we waste a lot of it."
-Seneca

The Weight of Expectations

Mira's desk looks like a battle map—brochures fanned out, mock tests stacked like barricades, a planner boxed with deadlines. Her phone lights up: rank screenshots, "got in!" celebrations, study flexes. Each ping tightens her chest. A sentence arrives dressed as certainty: If I'm not first, I'm finished.

She flips the phone over and stares at the same page three times. Nothing sticks. Then she writes one line on a sticky note: What's mine in the next 25 minutes? She sets a timer, chooses a single chapter, and starts. The room doesn't change, but the story does—slightly—back toward something she can do.

Pressure expands when attention clings to outcomes; it shrinks when action returns to the next controllable step.

Process Over Prize

Definition: Direct effort toward what you can do now—attention, preparation, integrity—rather than outcomes you can't command.

Teen Example: Master the next section; let the score arrive when it arrives.

Why the Pressure Feels Overwhelming

The culture around Mira hands her a script: success equals test scores, logos, applause. Feeds show highlight reels that look like normal life. Parents' hopes, spoken with love, mix with her own high standards until everything feels like a verdict. Comparison turns friends into mirrors that make her smaller.

She sketches two columns: "My lane" vs. "Everyone else's lane." The second column is endless and always moving. The first has six items she can actually do this week. Seeing it calms her. She hasn't solved admissions; she has made the next hours solvable.

Clarity beats noise; a path you can walk beats a race you can't finish.

Discipline of Assent

Definition: Don't believe every anxious thought—test for truth, usefulness, and alignment with values before agreeing.

Teen Example: Replace "If I don't get X, I'm nothing" with "I will give my best and live well either way."

Redefining Success

That night she writes her own definition: Success means living by wisdom, justice, courage, and temperance—learning deeply, treating people fairly, doing the right thing while scared, and keeping balance. Colleges can select; character is chosen daily. The shift changes small choices—less doom scrolling, more deep work; kinder messages; sleep protected like a class she can't miss.

When fear spikes, she rehearses the "no" for two minutes. If the email says no, I'll be sad, then meet my counselor Monday, refine Plan B, and keep building a life I respect. Fear softens when it sees a plan.

Outcomes matter, but virtues decide whether outcomes rule you.

Personal Success Standard

Definition: Measure life by effort, learning, and virtue—not by other people's lists.

Teen Example: Celebrate finishing the study blocks you promised, regardless of what others post.

Pressure Without Burnout

Application season peaks. The urge is to prove she cares by sacrificing sleep and joy. Instead, Mira builds a routine: three 25-minute focus blocks, two five-minute breaks, one 20-minute walk. She sets two windows to check results and mutes rank threads. She keeps sketching on Saturdays—an anchor reminding her she's more than a transcript.

Rejections sting; one acceptance lands with a grin she lets herself feel. None of them define tomorrow. The habits she practiced under pressure still fit after it. She learns she can strive without surrender.

Transition to lesson: Sustainable achievement grows from temperance—enough, not every last drop.

Temperance Guards Talent

Definition: Moderation protects clarity, energy, and joy so excellence can last.

Teen Example: One solid hour of work + sleep beats two bleary hours and burnout.

Practical Exercises

1) Success Redefined — Write a personal definition of success rooted in virtue and effort. Why it helps: Replaces borrowed goals with chosen ones.

2) Two-List Control — List "mine/not mine" before study or results. Why it helps: Redirects energy from worry to work.

3) 3-2-1 Workday — Three 25-minute focus blocks, two 5-minute breaks, one 20-minute walk. Why it helps: Sustains attention and mood.

4) Mistake→Method — After any test, log 3 wins, 2 gaps, 1 method change. Why it helps: Turns disappointment into a plan.

5) Comparison Fast — 48 hours without rank chats or acceptance posts. Why it helps: Resets attention to your own lane.

Reflection Questions

- How do you define success—by outcomes, effort, or something else? What would your virtue-based definition look like?
- When did pressure last spike, and how could the "two-list control" and a 25-minute start have helped?
- Which virtue—wisdom, justice, courage, or temperance—would most improve your approach this week?
- What one boundary (screen limit, sleep window, muted thread) would cut your stress in half?
- How will you celebrate effort daily, even when results are pending?

"Trade outcome obsession for virtue-driven effort—control what's yours, release what isn't, and let a life you respect be your measure of success."

Conclusion: Practical Action Plan for Continued Growth

Adolescence is a crucial chapter in the story of life—a time filled with challenges, discoveries, setbacks, and triumphs. As a modern teen embracing Stoic wisdom, the journey toward becoming your best self is ongoing. Growth is neither instant nor linear, but with steady effort and mindful practice, it is always within reach.

Here are key steps to guide your continued development:

Embrace the Dichotomy of Control: Focus energy on what you can influence and accept what lies beyond. This mindset frees you from unnecessary worry and empowers practical action.

Practice the Four Cardinal Virtues Daily: Wisdom helps you make sound judgments; justice guides your relationships; courage fuels your bold choices; temperance keeps you balanced. Let these virtues be your compass.

Master Emotional Response: Learn to recognize initial feelings without immediate judgment. Use pause, labeling, and reframing to manage powerful emotions constructively.

Build Self-Discipline: Cultivate habits that align with your goals, break tasks into manageable pieces, and use intention-setting to stay on track despite distractions.

Cultivate Patience: Tolerate uncertainty and delays with calm resolve. View obstacles as opportunities to grow endurance and deepen character.

Choose Friends Intentionally: Surround yourself with people who inspire growth and integrity. Set boundaries to protect your values and well-being.

Nurture Family Connections: Balance independence with respect and empathy. Communicate clearly and contribute actively to your household.

Develop Resilience: Face hardship with courage and grace, knowing challenges shape strength and wisdom.

Redefine Success: Prioritize effort, virtue, and learning over external achievements or comparisons.

Maintain Mental Discipline: Monitor and challenge your thoughts. Engage technology mindfully and cultivate an inner fortress of calm.

Remember, every day offers opportunities—a moment to act wisely, treat others fairly, stand courageously, and exercise self-control. Progress is made one choice at a time. Keep returning to these principles, and your character—and your life—will flourish.

Daily Stoic Practices for Teens: Morning and Evening Routines

Morning Routine: Begin with Purpose and Clarity

Set your intention: Before starting your day, ask, "What kind of person do I want to be today?" Pinpoint which virtue (wisdom, justice, courage, temperance) you will focus on.

Visualize challenges: Briefly imagine potential obstacles or setbacks you might face and how you can respond calmly and virtuously.

Affirm control: Remind yourself about the dichotomy of control: focus your energy on what you can influence.

Practice gratitude: Name 2-3 things you appreciate to foster a positive mindset before the day begins.

Mid-Day Check-In: Recenter and Refocus

Pause and breathe: Use a six-second pause to interrupt stress or impulsive reactions.

Assess control: Quickly ask, "What can I control in this moment?" Redirect your attention there.

Reframe thoughts: Replace catastrophic or negative interpretations with balanced perspectives.

Move your body: Take a short walk or stretch to refresh your mind and body.

Evening Routine: Reflect and Renew

Journal briefly: Reflect on your day with prompts such as: "When did I act virtuously? Where did I struggle? What can I improve tomorrow?"

Practice self-compassion: Acknowledge progress and accept imperfections as part of growth.

Revisit your intentions: Reinforce your commitment to the virtues and principles.

Prepare mentally for tomorrow: Visualize meeting upcoming challenges with resilience and wisdom.

Consistent daily practice builds habits, strengthens mental clarity, and anchors the Stoic mindset in real life.

Resources for Further Learning

To deepen your understanding and practice of Stoicism, here is a curated list of accessible resources tailored for teens:

Books:

The Daily Stoic by Ryan Holiday — Daily reflections and exercises grounded in classical philosophy.

A Guide to the Good Life by William Irvine — A modern introduction to living Stoically.

Letters from a Stoic by Seneca (Selected Letters) — Timeless wisdom in approachable letters.

The Enchiridion by Epictetus (Simple Translations) — Practical manual on Stoic practice.

Apps:

Stoa: Stoic Meditation — Guided daily meditations and philosophy explanations.

Daily Stoic Philosophy — Stoic quotes and exercises for everyday use.

Stoic Journal & Mental Health — Track moods and reflections to strengthen resilience.

Insight Timer — Free meditations including Stoic mindfulness content.

Websites and Communities:

DailyStoic.com — Articles, podcast episodes, and tools for applying Stoicism today.

ModernStoicism.com — Academic resources and global Stoic events.

Reddit r/Stoicism — Peer support and discussions centered on Stoic philosophy.

Philosophy Basics — Introductory philosophy materials with Stoicism sections.

Video Channels:

YouTube channels offering Stoic teachings and practical applications tailored to young audiences.

Using these tools and communities can support your ongoing journey into Stoic wisdom.

Acknowledgments

Writing this book has been a journey inspired by the resilience and courage of countless teenagers navigating the complexities of modern life. To the young people who seek wisdom amid the noise, who strive daily to be better versions of themselves, and who face challenges with strength—you are the heart of this work.

Gratitude goes to the teachers, parents, mentors, and friends who nurture growth, and to the ancient Stoics whose timeless insights light the path.

Thank you for allowing this philosophy to be part of your story. May it serve you well—for a lifetime of learning, courage, and flourishing.

***

https://my.clevelandclinic.org/health/articles/7060-adolescent-development
https://courses.lumenlearning.com/wm-lifespandevelopment/chapter/brain-development-during-adolescence/
https://pmc.ncbi.nlm.nih.gov/articles/PMC5074886/
https://pmc.ncbi.nlm.nih.gov/articles/PMC3705203/
https://www.aacap.org/AACAP/Families_and_Youth/Facts_for_Families/FFF-Guide/The-Teen-Brain-Behavior-Problem-Solving-and-Decision-Making-095.aspx
https://en.wikipedia.org/wiki/Peer_pressure
https://pmc.ncbi.nlm.nih.gov/articles/PMC6989808/
https://www.sciencedirect.com/science/article/pii/S1878929323000671
https://philosophybreak.com/articles/stoicism-and-emotion-dont-repress-your-feelings-reframe-them/
https://en.wikipedia.org/wiki/Stoicism
https://modernstoicism.com/stoic-philosophy-and-anger/
https://www.focusonthefamily.ca/content/dos-and-donts-of-helping-a-teen-after-a-breakup
https://www.oprahdaily.com/life/relationships-love/a63425048/how-to-help-your-teen-through-a-breakup/
https://www.youtube.com/watch?v=DU3I4UKOdfY
https://dailystoic.com/practical-stoic-exercises/
https://www.stoichandbook.co/ultimate-stoic-daily-routine/

https://mindfulstoic.net/how-to-practice-stoicism-an-introduction-12-stoic-practices/
https://counseling.northwestern.edu/blog/how-to-help-teen-experiencing-breakup/
https://www.fcps.edu/student-wellness-tips/peer-pressure

Write me up on rajatakre@gmail.com
Or for more books just check them on AMAZON.com

"Who am I?" 70 Questions to Self Enquiry

Book on Motivation

www.ingramcontent.com/pod-product-compliance
Ingram Content Group UK Ltd.
Pitfield, Milton Keynes, MK11 3LW, UK
UKHW011513190726
13845UKWH00034B/1236